JOHN THOMPSON'S
SUPPLEMENTARY PIANO COURSE

with

MELODY ALL THE WAY

A SPECIALLY DESIGNED COURSE FOR PIANO
MAY BE USED INTERCHANGEABLY WITH OR
SUPPLEMENTARY TO

THE MODERN COURSE FOR THE PIANO

BOOK 2-a

•

BASED EXCLUSIVELY
ON
WELL KNOWN AIRS

•

THE WILLIS MUSIC COMPANY
FLORENCE, KENTUCKY 41022-0548

Some interesting facts about

JOHN THOMPSON

HONORS CONFERRED

DOCTOR OF MUSIC DEGREE awarded for distinguished work in furthering Musical Education by means of his Piano Teaching Material.

FELLOW OF NATIONAL COLLEGE—Toronto, Canada.

TEACHER

DIRECTOR EMERITUS—Conservatory of Music, Kansas City, Mo.
Former DIRECTOR PIANO DEPARTMENT—Indianapolis Conservatory of Music.
Former VICE-PRESIDENT—Leefson-Hille Conservatory, Philadelphia, Penna.

CONCERT PIANIST

John Thompson has made two European Concert Tours and numerous American tours and has appeared as soloist with the following well-known orchestras:

London Symphony	St. Louis Symphony	Verdi Italian Symphony
Boston Symphony	Philadelphia Orchestra	Kansas City Symphony

COMPOSER

John Thompson's teaching material, in addition to its unrivalled popularity in the United States, is widely used in CANADA, the BRITISH ISLES, AUSTRALIA, NEW ZEALAND, countries in CENTRAL and SOUTH AMERICA and in far away CHINA. Special editions for some of these foreign countries have been printed. A number of his books have been transcribed and printed in Braille for the use of the blind.

LECTURER

His appearances, as lecturer have been hailed by thousands of teachers all over America.

CONTENTS

FOREWORD 4

PHRASING Three-Note Slurs

"Theme" .... *Kullak* 6

THUMB UNDER THE SECOND FINGER

"Waltz of the Fairies" .... *Schmitt* 7

THIRD FINGER OVER THUMB

"Amaryllis" .... *King Louis XIII* 8

SIGNATURE FOR FOUR-FOUR

"Elegy" .... *Massenet* 9

GRACE NOTES

"Rondo" .... *Mozart* 10

TWO-NOTE SLURS

"Song of India" .... *Rimsky-Korsakow* 11

LEGER LINES 12

LEFT HAND LEGER LINES

"Beautiful Minka" .... *Russian Folk Song* 13

DANCE FORM

"Polish Dance" .... *Scharwenka* 14

DOUBLE GRACE NOTES

"Gavotte" from Violin Sonata .... *Bach* 15

TRIPLETS

Theme from "Fifth Symphony" ...... *Tchaikowsky* 16

BOTH HANDS IN BASS CLEF

"Sorcerer's Apprentice" .... *Dukas* 17

THE PEDALS OF THE PIANO 18

LONG AND SUSTAINED PEDAL

"The Evening Star" .... *Wagner* 20

DANCE FORM

"Minuet" .... *Paderewski* 22

CONNECTED PEDAL

"Evening Peace" .... *Reinecke* 24

ESSENTIAL SUPPLEMENTARY BOOKS 25

STACCATO NOVELTY

"Funeral March of a Marionette" .... *Gounod* 26

ALLA BREVE

"Allegretto" .... *Haydn* 28

SCALES IN EXTENDED FORM 29

SMOOTH SCALE PLAYING

"Etude" .... *Streabbog* 30

CHORD STUDY

"Now the Day is Over" .... *Barnby* 31

THE SCALE AS MELODY

From "Sonata in C Major" .... *Mozart* 32

Theme from "Papillons" .... *Schumann* 33

CHROMATIC SCALE AS MELODY

"Valse Chromatique" .... *Godard* 33

LEGER LINES AND THUMB UNDER

"Mexican Hat Dance" .... *Folk Tune* 34

FINGER FLUENCY

"Valse" .... *Durand* 35

TWO CHORDS ON ONE ARM IMPULSE

"Soldiers' March" .... *Schumann* 36

THE SIGN FOR BROKEN CHORDS

"Spanish Dance" .... *Moszkowski* 37

SIXTHS FOR THE RIGHT HAND

From "Vienna Life" .... *Strauss* 38

SCALE FINGERING CHART 40

GLOSSARY OF TERMS, SIGNS AND ABBREVIATIONS 41

SUPPLEMENTARY SOLOS IN SHEET FORM .. 42

PROGRESSIVE SUCCESSION 43

CERTIFICATE OF MERIT 45

FOREWORD

This book, 2-a, progresses pianistically and musically from the point of development attained at the end of Book 1-b. As in the entire series entitled MELODY ALL THE WAY, examples are based almost exclusively on well-known airs. The advantages of this approach will have become apparent early in the series.

TECHNIC

Examples requiring the passing under of the Thumb—first under the second finger, then under the third, etc., are followed by pieces containing short scale passages. Use of the scale is shown both as melody and as accompaniment.

Assign the last half of the Hanon Studies (John Thompson edition) as this book is begun. This will train the pupil to combine the Touches already learned separately, thus supplying a wider choice of color effects.

THE PEDAL

The function of the Pedal is explained and examples are supplied which call for elementary use of the Sustained Pedal and the Connecting Pedal—both of which are described in detail.

RHYTHM

Since Dance Rhythms form the basis of so many musical compositions, it is advisable that the pupil become acquainted early with various dance forms. Consequently Book 2-a contains examples of the following dance and rhythmic forms:

Minuet	Valse (French)	Mexican Dance
Gavotte	Waltz (Viennese)	Polish Dance
Rondo	March (Military)	Russian Dance
	March (Funeral)	Spanish Dance

TECHNICAL BOOKS

The efficient teacher knows well the value—in fact, the necessity—of using supplementary books of technic. Technical works especially designed for correlation with this book are listed and described on page 25.

MUSIC WRITING BOOKS
(For home work)

Every worth-while teacher knows the value of Music Writing Books for home work. The author has designed three such Writing Books for the elementary pianist. The time of their assignment is a matter of individual preference on the part of the teacher but they should be used in the following order; THE NOTE SPELLER, THE SCALE SPELLER, and THE CHORD SPELLER.

GLOSSARY

A Glossary of all musical terms, signs and abbreviations used in this book will be found on page 41. The pupil should be required to refer to this page constantly until all definitions are memorized.

SUPPLEMENTARY SOLOS

A valuable item of the good teacher's equipment is a well chosen supply of suitable supplementary piano solos—either for recital or diversion. Page 42 lists a choice set of titles which will be found to complement this book admirably. This list will afford a ready reference for the busy teacher. The pieces have all been carefully selected, edited and fingered and are shown with explanatory notes on their teaching values.

THE PROGRESSIVE SUCCESSION

Information of particular interest to teachers will be found on page 43. Here is shown the inter-relationship of the various Thompson Books; how the Basic Books may supplement each other or be used interchangeably; where and when to use the books of Technic as well as a graded and classified list of books containing pieces.

CERTIFICATE OF MERIT

A Certificate of Merit has been included on page 45 as recognition of the successful completion of this book. It should be signed and dated by the teacher.

J. T.

PHRASING
(Right Hand)

Teacher's Note: The three-note phrases should be observed carefully in the following piece. The "Drop-Connect-Roll" attack, as well as all other fundamental touches, are fully explained in the *first half* of the John Thompson edition of the HANON studies—intended for use earlier in the course.

FOR USE WITH THIS BOOK

The *second half* of the HANON studies teaches how to combine the touches already learned, thus laying a foundation for Interpretation.

As this book is begun, the last half of the HANON should be assigned as supplementary material.

From
"Theme and Variations"

Moderato *Theodor Kullak*

THUMB UNDER THE 2nd FINGER

Hand in NORMAL five-finger position

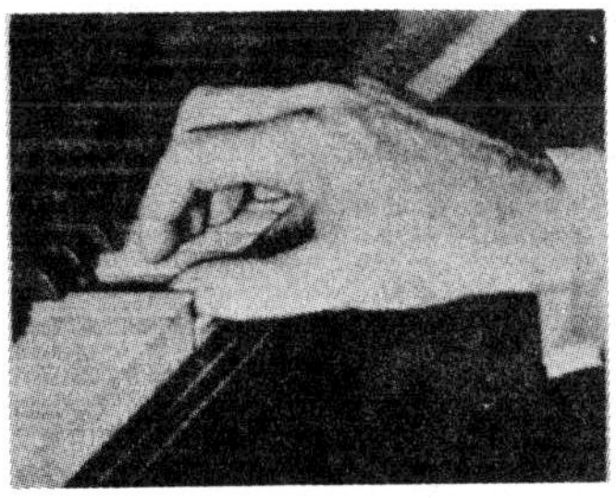

Hand position with thumb UNDER the second finger

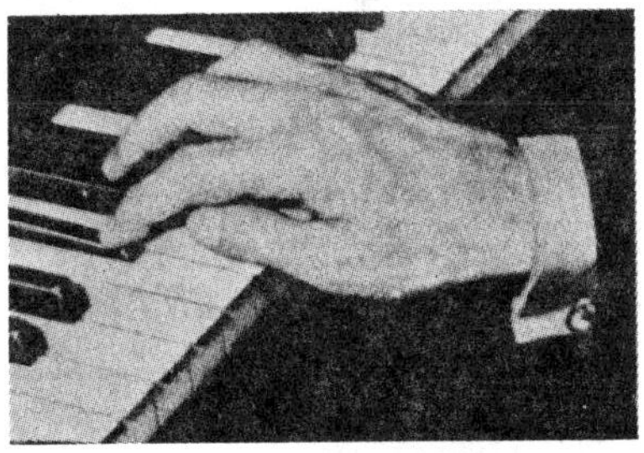

Before playing this piece place your hand as in figure 1 and practice the following exercise with the RIGHT HAND until the thumb can be passed under smoothly without turning the hand. The hand (or rather the arm) must pivot over on the thumb without breaking at the wrist.

From

"Waltz of the Fairies"

Allegro moderato

Schmitt

3rd FINGER PASSING OVER THUMB

The GAVOTTE is an old French dance which always begins on the third count and moves at a moderately fast tempo.

It has been said that the following Gavotte was composed by King Louis XIII of France. Its real origin is uncertain.

Be sure to make strong contrasts between legato and staccato and pass the 3rd finger over as smoothly as possible.

Observe all accents and keep an even tempo.

From

"Amaryllis"

Gavotte

King Louis XIII

SIGNATURE FOR FOUR-FOUR

JULES MASSENET was a French composer whose Operas were very popular even in his own day. They are still radio favorites. Among his most beloved works are "Thais", "The Juggler of Notre Dame" and "Manon".

The word ELEGY in literature, denotes a poem which is sad and touching. In this music of Massenet's we find the same feeling.

The sign **C** is used as a Time Signature to indicate 4/4. It is the modern version of the broken circle (which was formerly used.

In the following example play the left hand melody with the best possible singing tone and subdue the right hand accompanying chords. Pass the thumb smoothly under the third finger.

From

Elegy

Jules Massenet
(1842-1912)

GRACE NOTES

MOZART AND HIS SISTER PLAYING BEFORE MARIA THERESA.
From a Painting by [illegible]

MOZART, one of the world's greatest musicians, began composing little pieces at the age of four. And when he was six he played in public concerts.

There are several varieties of GRACE NOTES, but the one used most often looks like this 

It has no set Time Value and should be "flipped" into the principal note as quickly as possible.

Take care to phrase the two-note slurs properly and make a clear distinction between forte and piano in this little piece.

From

Rondo

Wolfgang Amadeus Mozart
(1756-1791)

Allegro

To Teacher: For list of supplementary solos in sheet form see page 42.

Every student knows this melody by Rimsky-Korsakow. It is popular on records and is played often over the radio.

Notice the use of two-note slurs in the melody—the same device used by Mozart so many years before.

Song of India

from the Legend "Sadko"

Rimsky-Korsakow
(1844-1908)

LEGER LINES

LEGER-LINES are *added* lines used above or below the staff.

An easy way to remember Leger Lines is to note the following:

LEGER LINES ABOVE THE TREBLE STAFF

The Leger Lines above the Treble have the same LETTER-NAMES as the spaces in the Bass.

LEGER LINES BELOW THE BASS STAFF

Leger Lines below the Bass have the same LETTER-NAMES as the spaces in the Treble.

LEGER LINES BETWEEN THE CLEFS

Leger Lines *between* the Clefs are *borrowed* lines. In the example below notice how the Treble Lines are *borrowed* to become Leger Lines in the Bass.

Middle C
Same in both Clefs.

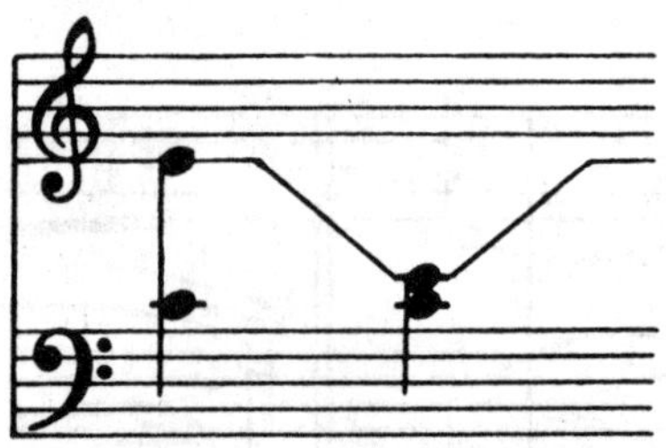

E } Here the E line of the
C } Treble is borrowed and used as a Leger Line in the Bass.

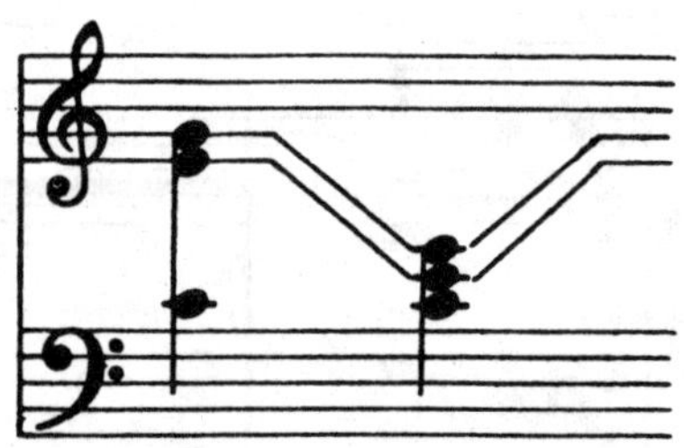

G } Both the E and G
E } lines are borrowed.
C

The same idea works *in reverse* when borrowing Bass lines to use as Leger Lines in the Treble.

Middle C

A and C

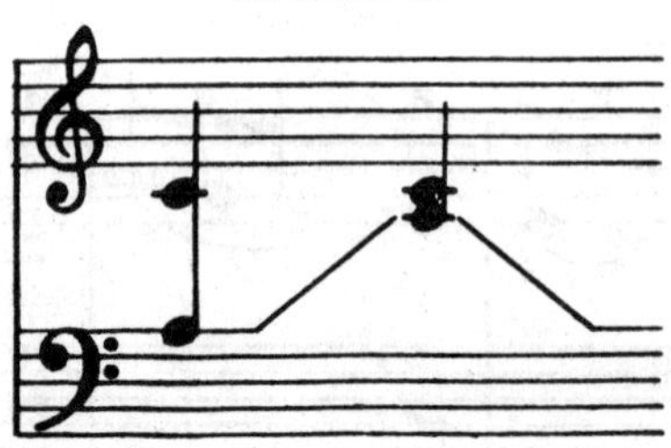

F, A and C

LEGER LINES
for the Left Hand

Be careful of the fingering and make sharp contrast between legato and staccato.

Beautiful Minka

Animato

Russian Folk Song

Be sure to observe the accents on the second beat and the sostenuto notes on the third beat of certain measures. Both are characteristic of Polish dance rhythms.

From

Polish Dance

Xaver Scharwenka
(1850-1924)

DOUBLE GRACE NOTES

JOHANN SEBASTIAN BACH came of a large family of musicians. He was one of the great masters of the art and showed signs of this genius when very joung.

The theme below is a piano arrangement of the Gavotte from the sonata for violin.

In this music we find DOUBLE GRACE NOTES which, like single grace notes, have no special Time Value.

Be careful to play the first grace note ON THE BEAT (together with the left hand chord).

Like this

Not like this

Morning Prayers in the Bach Family
(Painting by Rosenthal)
Courtesy Photographic Society, Berlin — N. Y. Graphic Society, N. Y.—Agen

From
Gavotte

Johann Sebastian Bach
(1685-1750)

TRIPLETS

PETER ILYITCH TCHAIKOWSKY was a Russian composer. He studied piano when a little boy, grew up to be a lawyer and then decided to make his beloved music his profession.

His six symphonies are popular in all countries but the 4th., 5th., and 6th. are best known.

A TRIPLET is a group of three notes (or chords) played in the same time usually given to two notes of the same value.

It is marked thus:

In the following example the three eighth notes in each triplet will be played ON ONE COUNT.

From

Symphony, No. 5

Peter Ilyitch Tchaikowsky
(1840-1893)

Andante cantabile

BOTH HANDS IN BASS CLEF

This music by Dukas is descriptive of the wild dance of an enchanted broom.

The story is from a famous poem called "The Sorcerer's Apprentice".

From

"The Sorcerer's Apprentice"

Allegro molto

Paul Dukas
(1865-1935)

THE PEDALS OF THE PIANO

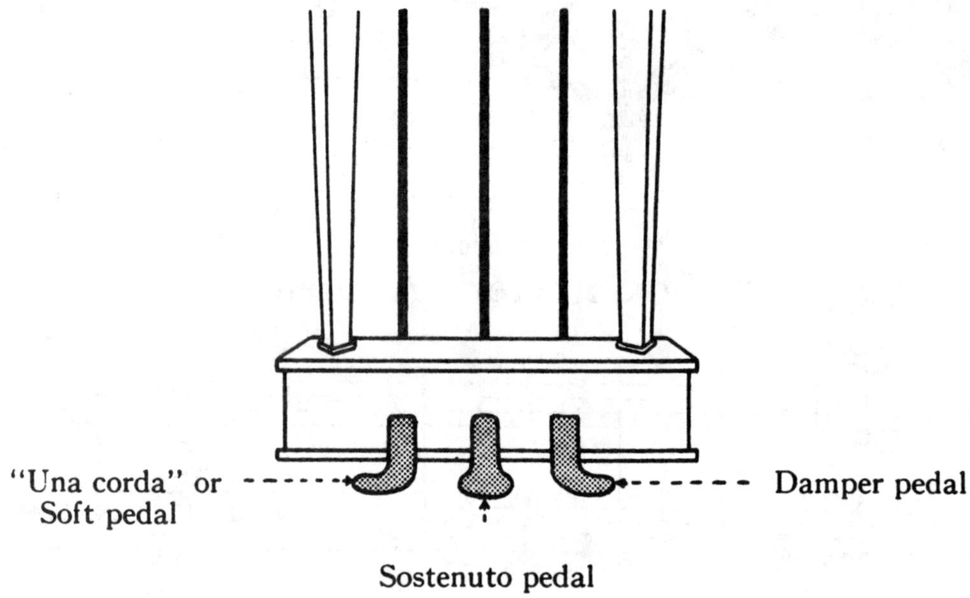

THE modern Grand Piano is equipped with three pedals. The pedal on the right is called the DAMPER PEDAL because when pressed down it raises up all dampers off the strings, thereby permitting all strings which have been struck to continue vibrating. In other words, *prolonging the TONE of strings affected.*

The pedal on the left is known as the SOFT PEDAL. It gives a softer and lighter tone. (Although it functions differently on Uprights than on Grands). It is usually indicated in music by the words "una corda."

The Middle Pedal (on all Grands) is called the SOSTENUTO PEDAL. It sustains only such keys as are held down at the moment the pedal is applied. In many Upright Pianos the Middle Pedal is constructed so that it may be used as a PRACTICE PEDAL. When in use, a strip of felt is lowered between the hammers and the strings, thus deadening the sound and also the quality of tone.

For the present, we shall study the use of the DAMPER PEDAL only. In the early part of the pupil's career it will be used for sustaining purposes but later on, it will be studied and used for color values as well.

There are many different signs to indicate when and where and how long to use the damper pedal but in this book the following sign will be employed throughout.

Play the following example, using the third finger. Apply the DAMPER PEDAL as indicated. LISTEN to the result!

(A)

Note how pleasant the sustained effect is to the ears!—because *all of the notes are related* and form a chord.

Now play the next example.
fingering and pedaling as indicated.

(B) 

This time the effect is blurred and very unpleasant because the notes are *not* related and form a series of dissonances annoying to the ear.

Play also the following examples. (C)  (D) 

It is evident to the ear that Example C is pleasant because only chords *of the same harmony* are sustained together.

Example D binds together, by the use of the pedal, chords that are different harmonies and the effect is a tonal jangle of harsh sounds.

It is quite obvious therefore, that great care must be used in applying the pedal. One's playing can be enriched or marred by its use. Fortunately, at this stage of advancement, it is simply necessary to follow the pedal markings strictly as indicated and correct results will follow.

THE SYNCOPATED PEDAL

The pedal should be applied, *not* at the moment the keys are being pressed down, but *immediately afterward.* The reason for this will become clear after the pupil has advanced further along the road to pianism. For the present it is sufficient that he form the habit of pedaling after the keys have been struck. This is sometimes called "syncopated pedaling." The following exercises will be found helpful.

EXAMPLE 1

Count "*ONE and TWO and THREE and FOUR and*" etc.
Pedal *down* on "and"—*up* on the numerals (1, 2, 3, 4)

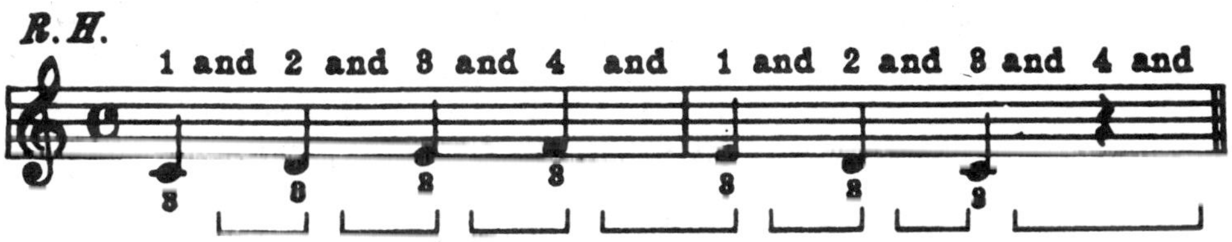

EXAMPLE 2

Count "ONE, TWO, THREE, etc.
Pedal *down* immediately *after* "ONE" in each measure.
Release pedal as you *say* "ONE" in each measure.

Teacher's Note: It is advisable to have pupils practice *left hand alone with pedal* in all examples employing pedal until its use becomes automatic and instinctive. This is particularly helpful because in the earlier grades the pedal is used mostly for the purpose of sustaining basses. Only the most elementary pedal effects should be attempted during the study of this book.

RICHARD WAGNER was born in Leipsig, Germany in 1813. He is considered to be the greatest of the Opera composers and he wrote the text as well as the music for his Operas.

First practice the broken chords without the low bass notes, thus;

When this can be done with ease, play the left hand alone including the bass notes. Then add the melody.

The Evening Star

from the Opera "Tannhauser"

Richard Wagner
(1813-1883)

Andante

Play the melody of this piece with your best possible singing tone.

Do not, under any circumstances, allow the melody to be obscured by improper use of the pedal.

Press down the pedal *immediately after* the note indicated by the pedal sign has been played, and release it sharply at the end of the sign.

Remember always that the use of the pedal can *make* or *mar* the composition.

W.M.Co. 6604

IGNACE JAN PADEREWSKI was born in Poland in 1860. He was probably the most popular of all concert pianists. The Minuet which follows was one of his early compositions. After World War I he became Premier of Poland.

Pay particular attention to the Rhythm—as always with dance forms. Use the exact fingering, especially where the Thumb goes under after playing the Triplet in the fourth measure.

From

"Minuet"

Ignace Jan Paderewski
(1860-1941)

Allegretto

mf
rit.
f a tempo
p

THE PEDAL IN CHORD PLAYING

IN the following piece the CHORDS should sound as though they were played on a church organ. This means that each chord must be as sustained as possible, that is, one chord must be connected to the next by means of the PEDAL.

NOTE THE NEW PEDAL MARK!

This sign is used to show that the PEDAL is released and pressed down again *immediately* in order to preserve an unbroken legato.

thus ⟶

Sometimes you will see a pedal mark like this ⟶

Or the word Ped. may be used like this ⟶

Always remember that all three markings have the same **meaning.**

From

"Evening Peace"

Carl Reinecke
(1824-1910)

ESSENTIAL SUPPLEMENTARY BOOKS

(A Page for the Teacher)

Since the technical needs of pupils vary so greatly, the wise teacher always assigns a book of technical studies and emphasizes the study of those exercises which tend to develop the phase of pianism most lacking in the individual pupil.

Listed below are two types of exercise material either of which is specially suitable for use with this book.

FIFTY SECOND GRADE STUDIES

By compiling a set of studies from all the well-known etude writers it has been possible to select only those written in happier moments and thus avoid the "exercise" flavor to which the average pupil objects so strenuously.

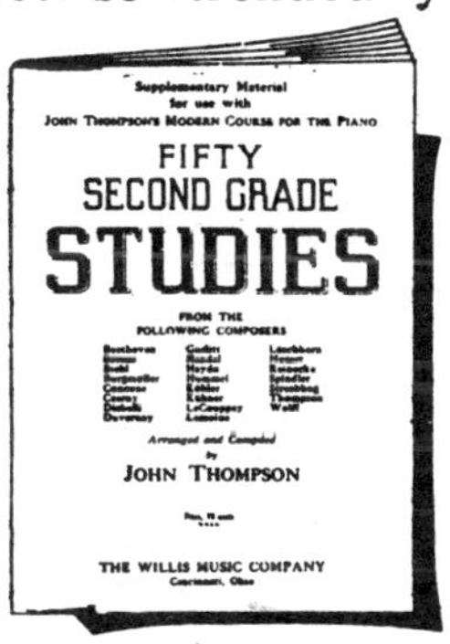

The book includes etudes from the following composers.

Beethoven	Gurlitt	Loeshhorn
Berens	Handel	Mozart
Biehl	Haydn	Reinecke
Burgmuller	Hummel	Spindler
Concone	Kohler	Streabbog
Czerny	Kuhner	Thompson
Diabelli	LeCouppey	Wolff
Duvernoy	Lemoine	

STUDIES IN STYLE

25 Tuneful Etudes for the Piano

As suggested by the title, these studies are designed to develop "style". They are the so-called "modern" type of exercise, tuneful and suggesting fragments from pieces.

The purpose of each exercise is printed at the top of the page. They are widely used throughout the country having attained popularity with pupils as well as teachers.

CHORD SPELLER

This Chord Speller by John Thompson was written to follow the Note Speller and Scale Speller, presumably used earlier in the course. Like its predecessors, the Chord Speller is a Writing Book for Home Work. It teaches how to write Major, Minor, Diminished and Augmented Triads. Inversions of Triads and how to recognize them quickly. Cadences and how to move the voices from one Cadence Chord to another. The Dominant Seventh Chord. The Diminished Seventh Chord.

STACCATO NOVELTY

Make a decided contrast between the staccato notes—which should be very brittle—and the sostenuto notes and short legato passages which occur occasionally.

Attack all accents sharply and abruptly. This treatment lends a bizarre effect to this little number which should be half tragic and half comic in character.

From

Funeral March of a Marionette

Charles Gounod
(1818-1893)

Allegro moderato

Charles Gounod was born in Paris in 1818 and died there in 1893. He was one of the outstanding French composers of his day and is perhaps best known for his Opera, "Faust", which is still popular. Excerpts from this Opera are frequently heard over the radio.

The "Funeral March of a Marionette" is a novelty written in one of Gounod's lighter moments. Originally scored for orchestra and later transcribed for piano, the adaptation used here was made especially for this book.

ALLA BREVE

In ALLA BREVE Time, indicated by a line through the signature thus, 𝄵 *, there are but TWO counts to the measure: one count to each Half Note. Learn it first in four-four Time, then increase the Tempo until you can play it counting two to the measure.*

From

Allegretto

Franz Josef Haydn
(1732-1809)

SCALES IN EXTENDED FORM

Thorough familiarity with scales means better keyboard technic

SCALES should now be practiced in extended form—that is, NOT DIVIDED BETWEEN THE HANDS.

Ascending C major scale — Descending C major scale

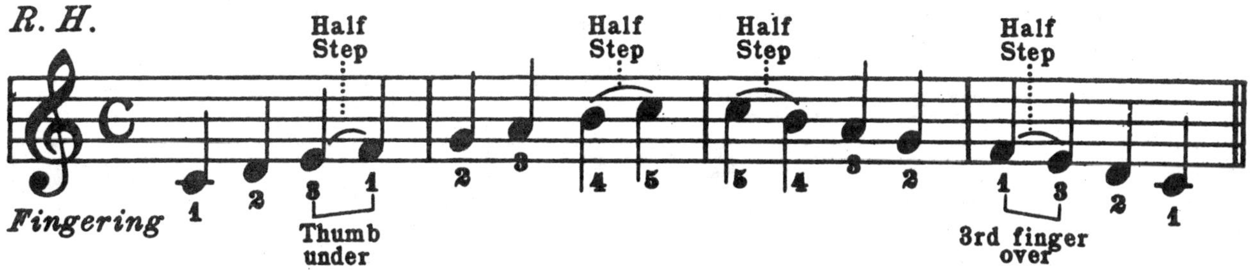

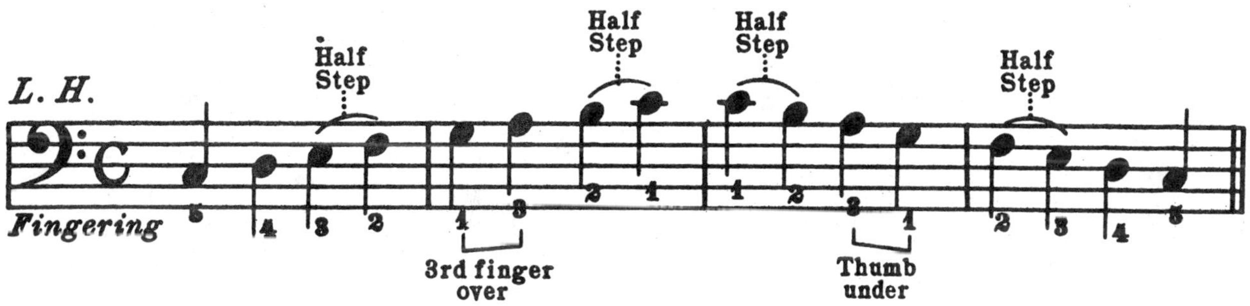

Rules and Guides for the fingering of all the scales are shown on the charts, page 40.
New scales should be studied at the direction of the teacher.

When the scale in extended form has been mastered, each hand separately, it is advisable to practice the hands together *first in contrary motion*, since this causes the *same fingers* to be used simultaneously in both hands. Later, they may be studied in parallel motion.

THE C MAJOR SCALE IN CONTRARY MOTION

THE C MAJOR SCALE IN PARALLEL MOTION

This is an exercise to develop smooth scale playing.
Observe the strictest legato and pass the thumb under with as little effort as possible.

Allegro moderato

Streabbog

CHORD STUDY

From

"Now the Day is Over"

Joseph Barnby
(1838-1896)

Andante moderato

To Teacher: For list of supplementary solos in sheet form see page 42.

From

Sonata in C Major

Allegretto

Wolfgang Amadeus Mozart
(1756-1791)

THE SCALE AS MELODY

From
"Papillons"

Robert Schumann
(1810-1856)

CHROMATIC SCALE (Used As Melody)

From
"Valse Chromatique"

Benjamin Godard
(1849-1895)

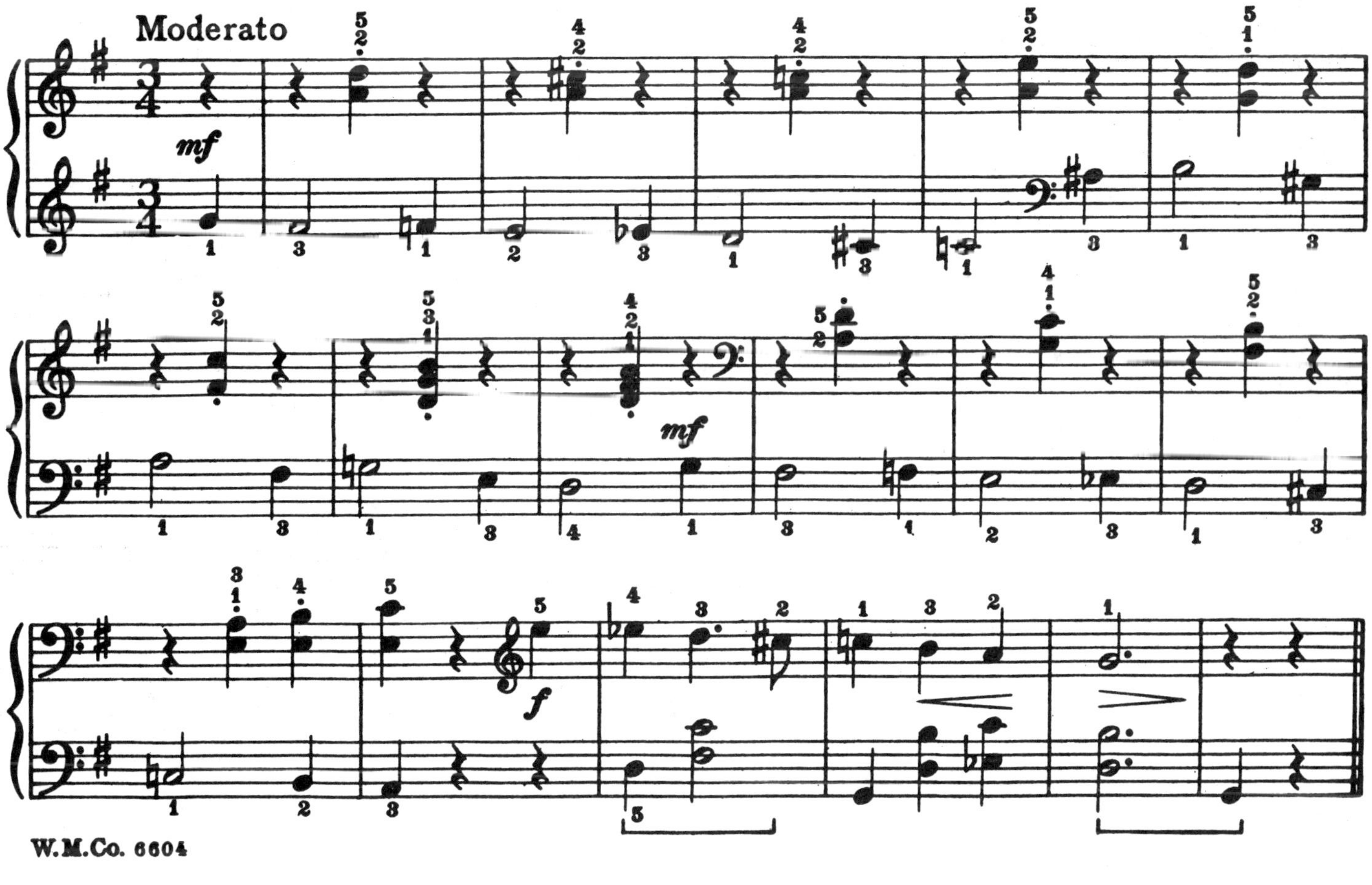

LEGER LINES AND THUMB UNDER

The chief feature of this number is its strongly accented rhythm.

Play the scale passages smoothly and apply sharp staccato touch to the left hand chords.

From

Mexican Hat Dance

Animato

Folk Tune

FINGER FLUENCY

In this piece the right hand is legato throughout against two-note slurs in the left hand.
Give a short touch of Pedal on the first beat of each measure as indicated.
Practice first at slow Tempo then increase the speed as finger fluency develops.

From

Valse

Vivo

Marie-Auguste Durand

PLAYING TWO CHORDS ON ONE ARM IMPULSE

When playing this March of Schumann's, use fore-arm attack. Where two chords appear close together (such as a 16th followed by an 8th) try to play both chords on ONE ARM IMPULSE.

Let the last chord of the pair be played a little more inward on the keyboard.

With practice you will learn to "bounce" from one chord into another on one arm stroke, which will help in producing a sharply defined rhythm.

Soldiers' March

Robert Schumann
Op. 68, No. 2

To Teacher: For list of supplementary solos in sheet form see page 42.

THE SIGN FOR BROKEN CHORDS

When a wavy line appears before a chord, it means that the chord is to be broken and played in the style of an arpeggio. Roll off the chords quickly so that the whole chord is heard ON THE BEAT without disturbing the even flow of the Tempo.

From

Spanish Dance

Animato

Moritz Moszkowski
(1854-1925)

JOHANN STRAUSS, known as the "Waltz King" was born in Vienna in 1804. He was a master of the Waltz form and wrote an astounding number of compositions, most of which are still popular.

Use wrist staccato when playing the 6ths in the following number. Take care to observe the two-note slurs over certain pairs of 6ths. Use the "Drop-Roll" attack exactly in the same manner as in playing single notes.

From

Vienna Life

Johann Strauss
(1804-1899)

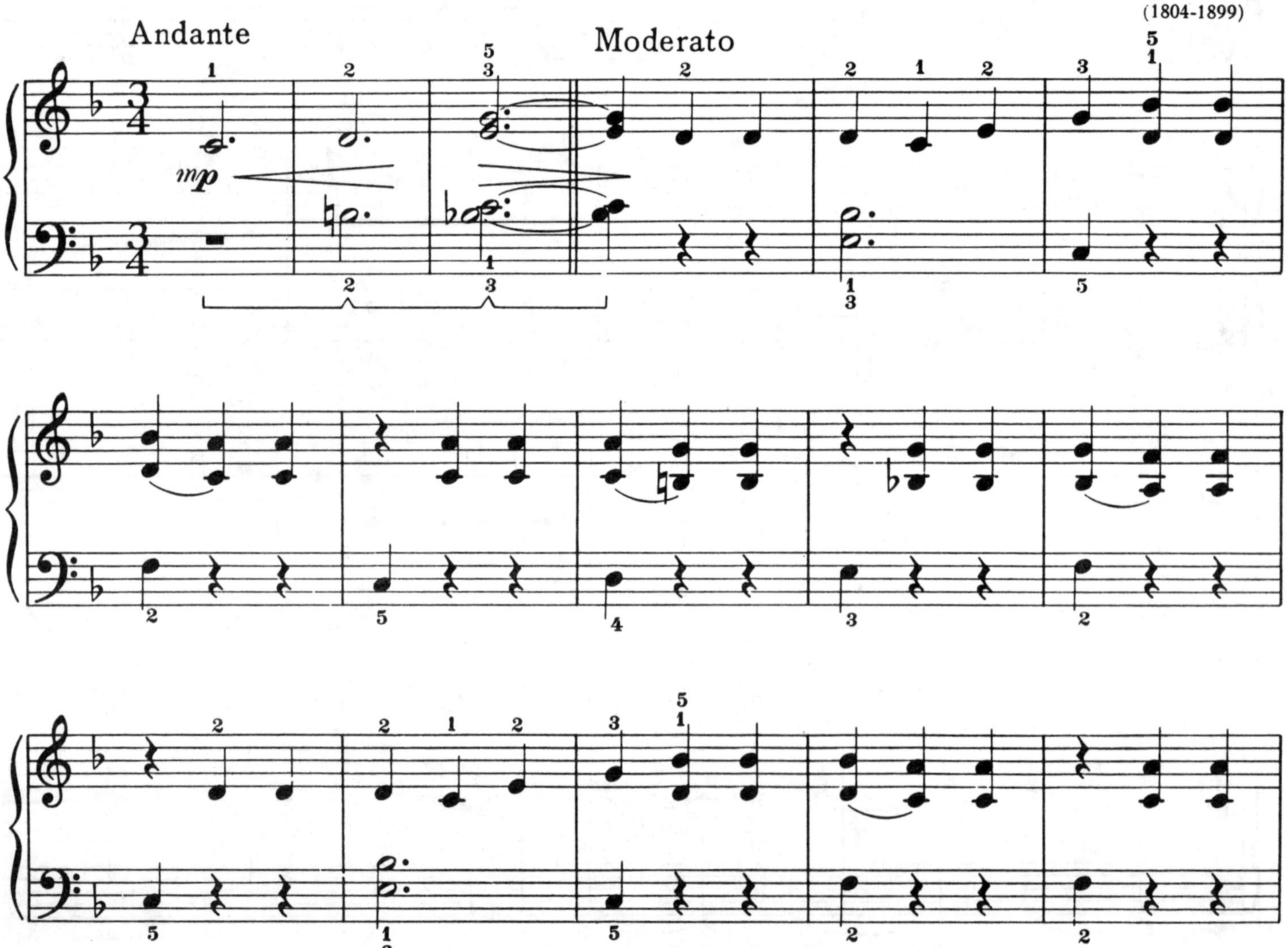

In Strauss' day and for a long while afterward old Vienna was famous as the gayest and most light-hearted city in the world. Strauss, by his genius, raised dance music to a higher level than it had ever reached before. He left to his beloved city and to the world a priceless legacy of deathless melody.

Viennese Ball-room scene from "April Blossoms" *Permission Metro-Goldwyn-Mayer*

Scale Fingering Chart

SCALES BEGINNING ON WHITE KEYS

Right Hand

The Thumb falls on the FIRST and FOURTH notes of the scale.

Left-Hand

The Thumb falls on the FIRST and FIFTH notes of the scale.

FINGER GUIDE
THIRD FINGERS OF BOTH HANDS ALWAYS PLAY TOGETHER.

There are two exceptions to the above rules— the scales of B major and F major. They are fingered as follows:

B MAJOR—*Begin with FOURTH finger in the left hand.*

F MAJOR—*End with FOURTH finger in the right hand.*

FINGER GUIDE
(for exceptional scales)
THUMBS OF BOTH HANDS **ALWAYS** PLAY TOGETHER.

MINOR SCALES

The WHITE KEY MINOR Scales are fingered exactly the SAME as the WHITE KEY MAJOR Scales.

SCALES BEGINNING ON **BLACK** *KEYS*

MAJOR SCALES

Right-Hand

Fourth finger on B♭ (or A♯).

Left-Hand

Fourth finger on the 4th note of the scale. Begin with THIRD finger.

There is one exception to the above rules— the major scale on G♭ (or F♯). For this scale use the rule of TWO'S and THREE'S, i.e., where TWO **BLACK** KEYS lie together, use the fingers 2 and 3. Where THREE **BLACK** KEYS lie together use the fingers 2, 3 and 4.

MINOR SCALES

B♭ MINOR, **E♭ MINOR** } *TWO'S and THREE'S in BOTH hands.*

A♭ (or G♯) M I N O R—*Fingered same as MAJOR.*

D♭ (C♯) MINOR, **G♭ (F♯) MINOR** }

Right Hand
FOURTH finger on the 2nd note of scale.

Left Hand
TWO'S and THREE'S.

GLOSSARY OF TERMS, SIGNS AND ABBREVIATIONS USED IN THIS BOOK

Abbreviation	TERMS	Signs
	Accent: Emphasize or stress	> ∧
	Alla Breve: Two beats to the measure—one beat to each half-note	₵
	Alla Marcia: In the style of a March	
allarg.	**Allargando:** A slackening of the tempo	
	Allegretto: Gay and moderately lively.	
	Allegro: Quick and cheerful.	
	Andante: Moderately slow.	
	Andantino: A little faster than Andante.	
	Animato: Animated.	
	A Tempo: Resume original speed.	
	Cadence: The end of a musical sentence.	
	Cantabile: In singing style.	
	Chromatic: Proceeding by half-steps.	
	Con Anima: With animation.	
	Con Brio: With brilliance.	
	Con Fuoco: With fury.	
	Con Moto: With motion.	
cresc.	**Crescendo:** A gradual increasing in tone. Shown also with the sign.	<
D. C. al Fine	**Da Capo Al Fine:** Return to the beginning of the piece and play to the end of the measure marked *Fine.*	
Dim.	**Diminuendo:** A gradual decreasing in tone. Shown also	>
	Dolce: Sweetly.	
Dom.	**Dominant:** The 5th degree of the scale.	V
	e: And	
	Espressivo: With expression.	
	Forte: Loud: Strong.	*f*
	Fortissimo: Very loud: very strong	*ff*
	Giocoso: Sportively.	
	Grace Notes: Little notes added as ornaments to give a graceful effect. They have no time value and should be played as quickly as possible	
	Grazioso: Gracefully: smoothly.	
	Leger Lines: Added lines above or below the staff.	
	Legato: Smooth and connected.	
legg.	**Leggiero:** Light, easy, nimble.	

Abbreviation	TERMS	Signs
	Maestoso: Majestic, grand.	
	Mezzo Forte: Moderately loud.	*mf*
	Mezzo Piano: Moderately soft.	*mp*
	Moderato: Moderately.	
	Molto: Much.	
	Non Troppo: Not too much.	
	Pause: To hold or prolong beyond the allotted time	𝄐
	Piano: Softly.	*p*
	Pianissimo: Very softly	*pp*
	Poco: Little.	
	Poco a Poco: Little by little.	
	Presto: Quick, nimble, rapid.	
	Reverie: A dreamy composition.	
rit.	**Ritardando:** A gradual slowing of the time.	
	Romanza: Romance.	
	Scherzando: Playfully, gaily.	
scherz.	**Scherzino:** A short composition in playful or whimsical style.	
	Semplice: Simply.	
	Sempre: Always.	
sfz	**Sforzando:** Forcing: the sudden accenting of a note or chord	
ten.	**Sostenuto:** Sustained. Indicated by a line over a note or chord	
stacc.	**Staccato:** Detached	
	Staccatissimo: Very short and detached	
Sub. Dom.	**Sub-Dominant:** The 4th degree of the scale.	IV
	Syncopation: Caused when accents fall upon weak beats, meanwhile supressing the natural accented beats.	
	Tempo: Time.	
	Tempo I: Resume original Time.	
	Tonic: The 1st degree, or keynote of the scale.	I
	Triplets: Three notes of equal value played in the time of two notes of the same value.	3
	Vivace: Lively, vivacious, light, gay.	
	Vivo: Quick, brisk, alive.	

JOHN THOMPSON'S STUDENTS SERIES

A carefully selected list of Teaching Pieces, suitable for use with Books 2-a and 2-b
of

"MELODY ALL THE WAY"

Title — *Composer* — *Key* — *Price*

BANJO PICKER, THE....Louise Wright........A...... .35
Staccato study; descriptive style. Easily memorized by means of "patterns"

BUSY CORNERS........Blaise Montandon....C...... .35
Humorous and highly descriptive with its traffic theme, automobile horns and several strains from "Reuben and Rachel" Excellent for finger legato.

BROWNIES' CARNIVAL..John Thompson......C...... .35
Legato melody and careful phrasing. A popular recital number.

CAPTAIN KIDD.........June Waldo..........Gm.... .30
A novelty which shows the Captain in a jovial mood as he dances the "Sailor's Hornpipe".

CHEER LEADER, THE...Irene Rodgers........C...... .40
A stirring march tune which exacts strict tempo and sharp rhythm.

DIRIGIBLE, THE........John Thompson......G...... .30
The balloon ascends and descends on a broken chord divided between the hands.

DREAMY-TIME SONG...William O. Munn.....F...... .30
Cute little cross-hand lullaby in which the clock strikes the bedtime hour.

DROWSY MOON........Lois Long............G...... .30
Theme in double notes in the right hand. Careful phrasing. Pedal ad lib.

FLYING PARADE.......E. L. Hopson.........F...... .35
A march through the clouds. Makes special appeal to "airminded" pianists.

HIAWATHA'S LULLABY.Willa Ward..........G...... .35
A beautiful number with true Indian characteristics. Two-note slurs in the right hand and a broken chord accompaniment in the left.

LITTLE GREENFEATHER
E. H. Blanchard......Gm.... .35
An Indian idyl. Fine study in style. Very musical.

LONGING..............J. J. Ames............F...... .30
A little tone poem which is "big" musically.

ON A SUMMER SEA....Ella Ketterer.........C...... .35
Cross-hand melody beginning in the left hand. Broken chords in slurred groups form the right hand accompaniment.

PARADE OF THE PENGUINS
Dorothy Wade........Am.... .35
A staccato novelty depicting the funny antics of these Antarctic creatures.

POMP AND PAGEANTRY
Hazel Cobb...........G...... .35
Fine chord study. Easy but sounds "big".

ROGUISH EYES.........Edmund Haines.......Em.... .30
A valse in modern vein, calling for sharp rhythm and careful phrasing.

SCHOOL BAND, THE....John Thompson, Jr...C...... .35
A typical band march in which the various instruments are cleverly imitated. A sure "hit", either in the drawing room or on the recital platform.

SPARKS.................John Thompson......Dm.... .30
Tuneful study in light staccato.

STAR-SPANGLED BANNER, THE
John Thompson......B♭..... .30
An easy arrangement designed for use in schools.

SWAN ON THE MOONLIT LAKE
Louise C. Rebe.......G...... .30
A little gem which develops melody playing in the right hand.

SWINGING HIGH AND LOW
Hazel Cobb...........D...... .30
A tuneful example of graceful rhythm and phrasing.

THEME FROM "LIEBESTRAUME" (Liszt)
John Thompson......C...... .30
Easy arrangement of this famous piano piece. Excellent study for Tone, Chord Playing and use of the Pedal.

TROOPERS ON PARADE
Evelyn T. Ellison.....C...... .30
A march highly descriptive of its military title.

UNDER SOUTHERN SKIES
Elizabeth B. Martin...C...... .40
Typical Southern dance tune which demands marked rhythm.

WOODS AT DAWN......Robert Nolan Kerr....F...... .35
An excellent trill study as well as a brilliant recital piece.

PILGRIM SUITE........John Thompson............. .60
A bit of American History told in music. Beautifully illustrated. Excellent for costume recitals. Contents: "Landing of the Pilgrims"; "Lullaby"; "John Alden and Priscilla"; "The Turkey Hunt"; "The First Thanksgiving"

ENSEMBLE PIECES

IN THE MORNING EARLY
Cora W. Jenkins......(4 hands).. .40

TULIP TIME.........Helen Broaddus......(" ").. .40

SPIRIT OF THE U. S. A.
Hazel Cobb...........(" ").. .40

THE STROLLING PLAYERS
Cora W. Jenkins......(" ").. .40

DOWN THE SHADY PATH
Cora W. Jenkins......(" ").. .40

FLAME VINE.........Mathilde Bilbro......(" ") . .50

BANJO PICKER......Wright-Lowenstein...(" ").. .40

TOY SHIPS..........M. Manning.(2 pianos, 4 hands). .40

Ask your dealer for a complimentary copy of John Thompson's GUIDE FOR PIANO TEACHERS
which shows musical excerpts from all of the above compositions

THE PROGRESSIVE SUCCESSION
of
John Thompson's Study Material for Piano

General Text	*Technic*	*Pieces*
TEACHING LITTLE FINGERS TO PLAY or MELODY ALL THE WAY (Preparatory book) ADULT PREPARATORY PIANO BOOK NOTE SPELLER (Writing Book)	TINY TECHNICS—Finger Drills based on well-known Airs.	TUNEFUL DUET ALBUM FOR THE FIRST YEAR. John Thompson, Jr.
THE FIRST GRADE BOOK (Modern Course for the Piano) or MELODY ALL THE WAY—Book 1-a followed by MELODY ALL THE WAY—Book 1-b SCALE SPELLER (Writing Book)	HANON STUDIES— Thompson edition (1st half)—To develop fundamental touches. FIRST GRADE ETUDES	FOR GIRLS WHO PLAY—Girl's book of pieces. LET'S JOIN THE ARMY—Boy's book of pieces. COVERED WAGON SUITE STUDENTS SERIES—Piano solos in Grade One
THE SECOND GRADE BOOK (Modern Course for the Piano) or MELODY ALL THE WAY—Book 2-a followed by MELODY ALL THE WAY—Book 2-b CHORD SPELLER (Writing Book)	HANON STUDIES—(last half) Combining touches learned in first half. STUDIES IN STYLE FIFTY SECOND GRADE ETUDES (Compiled)	PILGRIM SUITE WE'RE IN THE NAVY NOW—Musical journey 'round the World. STUDENTS SERIES—Piano solos in Grade Two.
THE THIRD GRADE BOOK (Modern Course for the Piano) AN INTRODUCTION TO BACH	THIRD GRADE VELOCITY STUDIES (Compiled) KEYBOARD ATTACKS	WORLD-KNOWN MELODIES — Album of 8 famous melodies. STUDENTS SERIES—Piano Solos in Grade Three.
THE FOURTH GRADE BOOK (Modern Course for the Piano)	FOURTH GRADE ETUDES (Compiled)	THEMES FROM PIANO CONCERTOS STUDENTS SERIES—Piano Solos in Grade Four.
THE FIFTH GRADE BOOK (Modern Course for the Piano)	FIFTH GRADE TECHNIC (Compiled) OCTAVE BOOK	STUDENTS SERIES—Piano Solos in Grade Five.

Note to teachers: **Be sure to ask for a *complimentary* copy of John Thompson's GUIDE FOR PIANO TEACHERS. It can be supplied by your dealer or by writing to the Willis Music Co., Cincinnati, Ohio.**

Manual 1 deals with Preparatory, First and Second Grades.
Manual 2 continues with Third, Fourth and Fifth Grades.
It has proven to be an invaluable aid to busy piano teachers.

Certificate of Merit

This certifies that

....

has successfully completed

BOOK 2-a

OF

JOHN THOMPSON'S

"MELODY ALL THE WAY"

and is eligible for promotion to

BOOK 2-b

....

Teacher

Date..